DIVORCE
THE
MODERN MAN'S
GUIDE

FIDEL BEAUHILL

CONKERPRESS

To Fidel,

"Happy Father's Day. Although we are no longer together, we do share and co-parent these beautiful girls. Fidel you are a great dad and stepdad and I feel blessed that we are able to work hard together to ensure they are happy, healthy and loved. Have a great day, when they finally roll out of bed"

Sharon (ex-wife)

PREFACE

As a mixed-race guy of divorced parents, I learned first-hand what a split feels like for a kid when it's done well. My dad, a strong Jamaican man, married my British-Brazilian mum who was, at the time, already a mother to 3 boys. That right there takes strength and courage. As a feminist woman with strong political views, she made sure us boys learned to stand proud in our own masculinity, while having the utmost respect for women. This was a blessing and it has served me well in life.

After the divorce my dad taught me the value of true and consistent parenting. Instead of having a full-time job, he chose to work part time; so that he could share in my upbringing. He moved close to us to be near me, and when we eventually moved to Bristol, he made sure that he saw me every other weekend. Never do I remember him talking badly about my mum. He was always, and still is, dignified in his conversation around family matters. This experience definitely helped me in handling my own divorce, parenting my kids and writing this book for you.

CONTENTS

DEDICATION

I dedicate this book to the most important people in my life now and always.

To Sharon my ex-wife: Thank you for our successful marriage.

To my mum: Thank you for giving me an appreciation of women whilst giving me pride in being a man.

To my dad: Thank you for teaching me how to think for myself, an appreciation for physical health and embedding in me the concept of being a Modern Man.

To my three princesses Chynah, Jasmine and Sienna: I will always be there when you need me.

And thank you to all of my family and friends who supported me through the divorce.

INTRODUCTION

If you are a woman going through a tough time, there are plenty of places you can go to for support. There are books, workshops and groups, both on and offline, where you can get the support you need to help you through … but you're not a woman, you're a man and, as men, we are largely forgotten when it comes to getting help during difficult times.

The common misconception is that because we are men, we're not in touch with our emotions. We are the stronger sex, the cavemen, the warriors, the conquerors and heroes, and so it's assumed that we don't need comfort and support and we can just tough it out. But if you're a man going through a divorce, then you know none of that is true because what you're most likely feeling is devastation. The effects of divorce are shown to be worse on the physical and mental health of a man than they are for a woman, and that is a proven fact.

A man feels the weight of responsibility deeply. It is in his psyche and it acts like a switch clicking on as he grows, finds a mate, and builds a family. That feeling of responsibility for earning and providing security for his family is primal stuff and the fear of not being able to deliver it is very real. If you're going through a divorce, or you're about to, this is all brought into the open and those feelings are poked and challenged, adding to the lack of control you may be feeling already. This is not my antagonistic view and it's never about us v them, it's about this … happy confident men and boys' equal happy confident women and girls, and we all need to do our bit to promote that.

In the beginning you will feel upset. Divorce is a loss and any loss is sad. You're losing your wife, your family and your whole way of life and this can have a devastating effect on how you see yourself now. It can also seriously affect your ego. Learning to deal with these feelings is important but, even in this day and age when you hear or see articles and information around the after-effects of divorce, the focus is mainly on the women and us men go unnoticed. But don't forget that marriage is a commitment made by two people and they are both responsible for it.

There are some options for men out there already, but we're going through a bit of a movement with these things and those groups tend to be run by enlightened men. This makes them all a bit hippy and a bit let's go out into the woods in stripy trousers and bang a bongo. That's not going to work for the ordinary bloke like me and you, and he is not going to don a pair of multi-coloured calf huggers for anyone.

The fact is, as a man, you will have to learn how to handle these feelings while at the same time leading your family through the divorce without the breakdown of those relationships. Without the drama and trauma that can affect you, your ex, and your kids for decades to come, if it's not handled properly.

This is about stepping into your masculine energy and taking the lead in your divorce for the wellbeing of everyone involved. The ordinary bloke gets that, which is why this book is for him.

"You cannot escape the responsibility of tomorrow by evading it today."

Abraham Lincoln.

1 CHAPTER ONE
TAKE RESPONSIBILITY

Responsibility

noun

the state or fact of having a duty to deal with something or of having control over someone.

"a true leader takes responsibility for his family and keeps them from harm"

Let's jump straight in … the modern man in marriage generally feels confident in his role. He is responsible for the family unit, for keeping it all together and running smoothly, and most of the time he does this without paying attention to little signs that things are not working. There are times when he does see the cracks in his marriage and, while he doesn't know what to do about them, he knows something has to be done. In either situation, when divorce inevitably comes knocking, the truth is it will be devastating for him.

In most cases taking responsibility is what you've already been doing. The house, the family, the finances and the expectations are all things you've been looking after. You've probably been juggling it well enough, but without realising it, you may have dropped the ball when it came to you keeping your masculine energy in the marriage mix.

In any great relationship the husband works together with the wife to provide the family with what they need. While the physical aspects of this are extremely important – the roof overhead, the food in the fridge, the bills paid etc. - the emotional side is equally as important but often lost in the responsibility you feel to provide. That certainly happened to me. I was focused on the dream that was pinned to my vision board. The big house, the countryside, the cars, the horses … but it wasn't my dream and while I was focused on my responsibility to provide for it all, the energies in my marriage were shifting and I didn't see that until it was too late.

If you've got to the end of the road and divorce is inevitable, there is no point dwelling on how you got there, whose fault it was or what you could have done to prevent it. What is important now is taking the lead and this is not about aggression or dominance; this is about guiding everyone safely through to the other side of your divorce so that the future relationships between you, your ex and your children remain intact, as do all of you. This is the time for you to take responsibility for the future.

If things deteriorate and your wife starts getting angry

or spiteful, it's normally because she doesn't feel safe. If you're experiencing this, step into your masculine energy and be considerate and kind throughout the process and it will help prevent this.

Your role as a husband is going to change to that of an ex-husband, but your role as a man remains the same. As a man, it's your job to take the lead.

Think about when you first started dating, when you were wooing her. Then you would have been full into your masculine and she would have loved that. What can happen when you get married and the kids come along is that you try to make her happy, and in doing so you start asking her what she wants rather than just doing and, in the end, she is making all the decisions. You are thinking, well if I just do what she tells me to do, that will make her happy, but that's where the energy shift starts and if it continues like that throughout your marriage, she will think where the f*ck has my man gone. You might not notice this shift at first, as outside of the house, you're still in the same energy as you've always been. If she is also out at work, this can be a contributing factor, as in the workplace, women often step into their masculine energy. There is nothing wrong with that – the workplace is a competitive place and to get ahead, she may sometimes feel that she has to do it. This can also cause problems in the marriage and a lot of the time, it's when the sex stops.

If you looked at the run up to this point, you'll often see times where the masculine and feminine energies between you and your wife shifted. Times when she made the decisions and took the lead, and while this most definitely did not happen overnight, it would have contributed to the situation you find yourself in now. This divorce was on its way when that started.

Now is about stepping into your masculine. The masculine and feminine energies are within us all and we use both of those resources as we go about our daily lives, but it's within our family and our romantic relationship where it's most important for the man to remain in his masculine and the woman her feminine, because that keeps the sexual polarity aligned. If that starts to shift, it can upset the entire relationship and definitely be a contributing factor to divorce.

If you're getting a divorce, it's likely that somewhere during your marriage your wife stepped into her masculine energy and you leaned too far into your feminine and over time, this will have created an imbalance in your relationship. She would have become the leader in the family and if that has happened, we need to work on shifting the balance and getting you back in charge, so that you can now lead the way through this divorce.

When you look into the statistics here in the UK, you'll find that it's mostly women who instigate divorce (stats were 66% in 2018 for instance). When this happens and the wife takes control, it is common for the man to abdicate responsibility for leading his family through this challenging time because he feels like he is not needed. Some men run away; not necessarily physically, (although that can happen) but more often mentally or emotionally and in doing so, they become more vulnerable and their family unit more unstable.

If you want to prevent this from happening, it's crucial to identify it first. You can do this by becoming more self-aware, which will give you the opportunity to turn it around, step into your masculine energy and take responsibility. When you do this, you can take your rightful place as the leader of your family and do all that is needed. This is not only for the duration of the divorce, but for the interwoven relationships you will all have in the future.

Becoming self-aware will help you become a grounded and decisive leader. Be honest with yourself about your behaviour and the choices you made, and also acknowledge and accept the part you played in the breakdown of your marriage. This is vital, cathartic and empowering.

If it was your ex who lied or cheated, if she was abusive or it was her who instigated this divorce, you still can't put all the blame on her because, at the very least, you made the choice to be with her in the first place, and you stayed as long as you did. I know this is an overused and tired analogy, but it really does 'take two to tango'.

Take an objective look at the relationship you had, then accept some responsibility for your part in it. Focus on your own behaviour and how it contributed to the breakdown. This will prevent you from falling into victim mode, which is dangerous as it will spread to other areas of your life and affect how you judge things. You'll find yourself with all kinds of problems in your personal and working relationships when you slip into your victim brain.

It will also make your recovery from the divorce process longer and, trust me, it will be a recovery. If you don't take your time and do all of this properly, it can go so deep that you won't fully heal, and you'll end up feeling completely disempowered.

Think about this logically. When a man is in the victim state, he comes across as needy, which most women find absolutely repellent. Being needy will also most likely drive your ex further away and cause her to raise her defences in order to protect herself. If that happens it can cost you financially and emotionally and that's something you really want to avoid.

You've got to do the work on yourself first and then you can shed the victim role and step into your empowered leader, both mentally and emotionally. This is good for you and your family, making it a win-win all round. It all starts with you taking responsibility and leading your divorce by initiating the process and if that hasn't happened already, you need to open up communications with your wife and have the first of many potentially difficult conversations. Here are some of my best tips to help you do that:

TIMING

Divorce is a marathon not a sprint. Getting the timing right is important and even though you may feel like you need to get it all off your chest now, you've waited this long already, so be patient. Think about damage limitation too as the conversation is going to be the equivalent of dropping a bomb on the family home. Even if your partner has an inkling that something is coming, nothing can prepare her for the words

'I want a divorce.'

If you blurt that out in the middle of a row or stressful situation, there will be carnage. Wait until you are both in a good place before saying those words because you'll need to be emotionally able to cope with the fall out.

DO

Make sure you allow time and space for her to respond appropriately. You need adequate time for this conversation, so don't do it just as you're leaving for work. Try to remain calm, ask questions and stay in touch with your emotions.

DON'T

If the kids are at home and wandering around, or in the lounge watching a film, don't pull your wife to one side in the kitchen for the conversation. You really don't know what her reaction will be, and it won't be fair on your kids if all hell breaks loose. Especially if they witness it all. Don't do it in public either. I know you may think if you do it in a public place, she won't create a scene, but even if you're right, you'll have to go home at some point. Doing it that way is a mistake and it will set the tone for the divorce itself.

If you happen to be in couples' therapy already, then that is a good place to bring it up as you will have professional support to guide you both through the process and the therapist can mediate and give you guidance on how to move forward.

PLANNING

Think about the words you're going to use and plan out what is best to say. Don't use accusatory language or start laying the blame at her feet as she will raise her defences and most likely retaliate. Before you know it, the conversation can spiral out of control and nothing useful will come from that. Any sentence that starts with: 'You should' or 'You don't/didn't', is like prodding her viciously in the head with your finger.

Instead, point that finger back at yourself and tell her openly and with honesty how you feel, explaining why you believe a divorce is the right decision.

Try to be as clear and precise with your words as possible and don't give her the impression that the door is still open and there is a chance of rekindling the relationship. If there is the slightest possibility of that in your mind, then don't have the conversation at all, but if your mind is set then now is not the time to be vague, ambiguous or give her false hope. When you speak, be understanding and talk about how you think she might be feeling. Be considerate and caring and do listen - it's likely she hasn't been happy either or at the very least, she will know that you haven't been and that will have caused her to feel unsafe, unsure and frustrated.

When you're planning, be practical and draft out some of the important points, then practice how you're going to say them. You'll find that this gives you deeper clarity around the situation and that will be really useful when the time comes.

KEEP IT SIMPLE

This is the first of many conversations you two will have as you work out the details of the divorce. It's not something that can be finalised in one conversation and this initial talk is to open up the subject and tell your wife you want a divorce. It's not the time to get into the details around child arrangements or financial specifics, as these can be overwhelming for you both at this stage and the pressure of it can easily take it from talk to argument. You'll both say things you'll regret, and this will make the next conversation much harder than it could be.

It's ok to talk about wanting a harmonious process where you both choose to put the kids in the centre, rather than the middle of your divorce (more on this later) and how you don't want it to turn into a war zone, just don't get bogged down in the finer details or any negotiations at this stage.

Once you've had the conversation you can instigate the legal process. I mentioned earlier that the majority of divorces are instigated by women and if this is what's happening to you, it's not too late to take back control and put yourself in a position to lead. Starting the legal process is a necessity, but it's not my expertise and I won't be talking much about it here, other than to say, there are plenty of places you can get that advice and it's important to do so.

To get yourself ahead of the game, get the legal advice, but also plot out a timeline of where you are now and where you want to be at the end of it all. Stick to that process as you go.

This is a subject that crops up a lot in my men's group and the guys talk about how they have come out of the divorce worse off in regard to finances and the children. While it's not always the case, this can be due to them having been passive or reactive during the divorce process and that behaviour allowed their ex-wife to take the lead and dictate the way.

If you're the one making the first move, you stand a better chance of controlling the energy and the mood of your relationship and I cannot stress enough that it's in your best interest to evoke peace, love and teamwork. The only winner in a bitter divorce war is the solicitor.

Let me be clear here. When I say take the lead, I don't mean that you make decisions to piss her off. I don't mean that you act aggressively in pursuit of everything you want, and I don't mean that you try to get the kids on your side. What I do mean is that you consider the outcome for everyone involved and then make decisions for the greater good. Of course, this is all well and good if your ex is being rational and reasonable, but I'm aware that a lot of men are not so lucky. Whatever your personal situation, staying in your masculine throughout this divorce will lead to a better outcome all round.

SOME THINGS TO THINK THROUGH

- Have a bloody plan.
- Get legal advice.
- Know how much it's going to cost you.
- Where will you both live in the short and long term?
- How will the childcare arrangements work?
- How is this going to affect your work?
- Can you take some time off work?
- Have you got family events or holidays booked? How are you going to cancel or manage those?

If you've been reading and it's slowly dawning on you just how emotionally passive you've become, then this book may be the slap around the face you need. Let it empower you into taking responsibility for the situation. A divorce is never going to be all rainbows, but by realising and utilising your inherently masculine traits, you can make it less turbulent for all concerned … including yourself.

Being the modern man in your divorce means still being responsible for your family unit and keeping everything together as you all transition into a new way of living. Make sure you are in your masculine energy and use it for the good of everyone.

"Quick decisions are unsafe decisions."

Sophocles.

2 CHAPTER TWO
DON'T ACT ON YOUR EMOTIONS

Emotion

noun

a strong feeling deriving from one's circumstances, mood, or relationships with others.

"he made himself ill by trying to hide his emotions"

If you had a marriage like most men, there would have been moments of anger and conflict, which is normal. It's never nice but it can be beneficial if you both learn and grow from it. The best kind of relationship is where your masculine and feminine energies complement each other and work together, but all marriages will go through turbulence at times. The couples who last the longest will ride it out together, but when arguments happen and you let them drive a wedge between you, inevitably the gap gets wider, the energy shifts between you and the marriage falls into a downward spiral.

The fact is, divorce can easily turn into a battleground and, as a man, you will find it far easier to battle over the kids or the furniture than you will to battle your own emotions. If you take all of your shitty feelings and channel them into a fight with your ex, you'll feel more in control and more vindicated perhaps, but it's really not how you win this battle. To come out victorious in divorce is not about battling but by leading the members of your family through it unharmed.

Men and women experience conflict differently. A woman tends to be more lenient and she will take into consideration your feelings around what you're saying. This doesn't mean women don't get angry, because, of course, they do. It's the thinking process of men and women that I'm talking about here and this is the idea behind books such as 'Men are from Mars and Women are from Venus'. We just think differently from each other and that's all there is to it. If the breakdown in your marriage came from the chipping away of these emotions, then it is really important that you don't let the divorce go the same way.

Divorce is not usually a happy subject and it will bring up many emotions including anger, fear and guilt, among others, and if your marriage has kicked along in this way for a long time, then you'll be carrying a lot of that forward. In situations like this, the intense emotions can be responsible for you making rash decisions and you want to avoid those at all costs as they are the ones you'll regret.

There are actually 5 main negative emotions around

divorce, and you will probably feel all of them as you transition from married man to single man. You can try to resist but whether you want to feel them or not won't matter, as they will come. Learning to process them in the right way is important and it will be beneficial for you but just remember that your feelings will change frequently dependent on each situation and if you decide to react and retaliate, it won't help anyone.

Anger, hurt, fear, guilt and sadness are normal and necessary even, but it's not ok to let them control your communication or decision making, as now is the time to be in control ... clinical even. The minute you respond in an emotional manner you will create emotional situations.

There are many reasons for divorce, but if your marriage started to break down when your wife began to make the majority of decisions, that was her stepping into her masculine energy and she will jump straight back into it if she thinks you're not capable of doing the job properly. It's really not that she wants to, but her experience is telling her she needs to, because you won't.

Whatever the situation is and no matter how volatile, or how much it is pushing your buttons, if you learn to press your own pause button, it will change everything. It will give you the space and time to think clearly and to put a plan together for the future to make sure you know how to handle the whole thing. You wife knows you really well and she knows what buttons to push to get a reaction, so just remember that you DO NOT have to respond to everything straight away.

Take the time you need to process these emotions as they arise and don't let them define you.

ANGER

Everyone gets angry and there are many reasons around a divorce that can make you feel that way. It's a human emotion and it is ok to feel it, but what's not ok is to share it when you're in it, as that's when it creates more problems and when it will have a very big impact on your kids. Sometimes we get so angry that we don't know how to deal with it, and we can't express it in responsible words, so it becomes verbal abuse instead. If you have poor anger management at this critical time, it will cause problems for everyone, and continue to do so for many years to come.

Suppose you get an angry message from your wife and it stirs you up so much that you feel your anger rising. Is now really the best time to send a message back to her? It's much better to wait until you've calmed down a bit and if it was a text message, read it again and make sure you're reading it how she meant it. Look at it again, could you be adding something that's not there? Texts are notoriously misconstrued and even the wrong punctuation can make something with a good intention sound bad. People often text when they are busy and don't really pay attention or think about the way you will read their message, so they can be easily misinterpreted. Even if it was an angry message, you sending a reactive response to your estranged wife's bitter tone is only going to make things worse.

HURT

Hurt people hurt people. That's a saying and a truth. When we're hurting, we can lash out and that comes from a place of pain. When we're in pain it can feel like we've been attacked and the primal response to an attack is to try and defend ourselves in the same manner. People often lash out in pain.

There are bound to be times that are really painful as you navigate your way through your divorce. You and your wife have been left with a gaping hole where the attachment was, and you may be surprised at the rawness of emotion you feel. This pain is not organised or structured and it's definitely not polite, as it will call on you at the most unexpected and unwanted times. It can be absolutely exhausting and also strangely gratifying as if holding onto it gives you a kind of lifeline.

FEAR

Fear and anxiety can join together at the early stages of divorce. The thought of everything changing causes anxiety and this escalates into fear when you start to think about your home, your children, your finances, your relatives and even your joint friends. If you could think about each one at a time it wouldn't be so bad, but sometimes you open the box and they all come spilling out making you feel overwhelmed and fearful. When you're feeling that way, you may start thinking that you've made a mistake.

Was your marriage really that bad?

If you got back together, knowing what you know now, wouldn't it be better?

Should you give it another go?

We all think like this. It's just part of the process but making an impulsive decision out of fear will put you and everyone else in a much worse position in the long run.

The more you think into the future with a negative mindset at this stage, the worse it will get. The fear of being alone or thinking you'll be ostracised by your mutual friends. The fear of not being able to support both the households and not seeing your children enough. The fear that you're not capable of seeing this through or even worse, that no one else is going to want you in the future.

Try to understand these thoughts for what they are and not let them debilitate you.

GUILT

Many men divorce and then walk away with nothing for themselves because they feel guilty. It's as if they make the choice to suffer as a way to appease the guilt inside of them. These men may leave the big house and everything in it to their wife just to feel better and if they do make all of their decisions from a place of guilt, it will end up costing them hundreds of thousands of pounds. This may initially make them feel better but eventually they will regret it. If you've been thinking this way or you feel tempted, remember that you can't turn back the clock, so don't rush anything. Take the time to think everything through and remember to pause.

As a parent you'll probably be feeling guilty about the effect this is going to have on your kids and how it's disrupting their life. Thinking that your actions will have a negative effect on their future can lead to hesitation about the divorce and you overcompensating for it.

Overcompensating is also a mistake that is driven by feelings of guilt and this can make it feel like the right thing to do at the time. Trust me, it won't be. Take the advice of someone who has been through it and when you feel any of these emotions, stop, hit the pause button and don't make any rash decisions.

SADNESS

Who says it's not ok to cry? If it wasn't, do you think you'd be able to do it physically? Crying is about being human, not being female. When you feel sad you need to release that sadness and it's good to do it in your safe space (more on this later). A divorce is one of the most stressful events you will ever deal with in life and this makes it easy to slip into sadness and even depression, especially if you try to suppress your emotions.

As you navigate through this divorce you will run through the whole range of emotions, but don't run from them. And don't try to stop or hide them either. Instead learn to confront them, understand them and find ways to process them. When you don't process your emotions properly, the danger is that revenge will become a part of your thinking. This will bring out the shadow feminine energy and the result is an absolute 'shitstorm'. You will find yourself trying to cause trouble for your ex by being mean and spiteful and this can lead to passive aggressive behaviour. The masculine is a physical energy which can result in abuse, anger and violence, which are all things to be avoided. You can waste a lot of energy trying to get revenge on your ex and looking for things to cause trouble about.

When you're looking for payback, what you're actually doing is not focusing on the important stuff. The inner work that we must do on ourselves if we're to move on. Hanging around in this state will cause you to focus on the wrong direction instead of taking care of yourself and your kids and while you're fixated on trying to tear her life down, you're not building yours.

This can get really tricky if you find out your wife is dating someone new and you've not managed to process your emotions. If you don't learn how to do this, you can easily spiral into unhealthy behaviours.

'We need to rebrand vulnerability and emotion. A vulnerable man is not some weird anomaly. He is open to being hurt, but also open to being loved.

Grayson Perry

3 CHAPTER THREE
BE VULNERABLE

Vulnerable

adjective

exposed to the possibility of being attacked or harmed, either physically or emotionally.

"his vulnerability gave him the courage to lead"

We men are emotionally complex and most of us grew in an environment that trained us to avoid or hide our feelings. Vulnerability is often seen as negative for men and mostly associated with the female of the species, but if you can remember when you first fell in love, then you will understand the vulnerability I'm talking about. As a man in love, there really is nothing you won't do in pursuit of your woman which leaves you completely exposed, but you don't care because your sole aim is to win her heart at any cost. Think about Will Smith in 'Hitch'. He stands in the street, pouring his heart out to Eva Mendes while she is standing with another man. That is beautiful and brave, but can you see how vulnerable it makes him? If you remember when you first fell in love, then you already know how to be that kind of vulnerable yourself.

Incidentally, if you can tap into this vulnerability and keep it alive in a relationship, your next one will be your last one. We'll talk more about that in my second book…

There is a general misconception around being vulnerable in that it means weakness. But that's not true. Being vulnerable in a relationship is about having the courage to show your emotions, and this can be your greatest strength. It's about standing up and being true to yourself and your feelings, even when you know you may get knocked down in the process. That is brave.

Even the most manly of men, like James Bond, are not exempt from vulnerability. Bond may be a fictitious character, but the world has bought into him and his personality, and he serves as a prime example of the type of man women want to be with. It's an unrealistic expectation and we can't all be James Bond, but there is a paragraph in 'Casino Royale' which links us all as men.

'Above all, he liked it that everything was one's own fault. There was only oneself to praise or blame. Luck was a servant and not a master. Luck had to be accepted with a shrug or taken advantage of up to the hilt. But it had to be understood and recognised for what it was and not confused with a faulty appreciation of the odd, for, at gambling, the deadly sin is to mistake bad play for bad luck. And luck, in all its moods had to be loved not feared.

Bond saw luck as a woman, to be softly wooed or brutally ravaged, never pandered to or pursued. But he was honest enough to admit that he had never been made to suffer by cards or by women. One day he would have to accept the fact, he would be brought to his knees by love or luck. When that happened he knew that he too would be branded with the deadly question-mark he recognised so often in others, the promise to pay before you have lost: the acceptance of fallibility'

Ian Fleming

Even James Bond knew that one day he would be completely vulnerable and exposed by love.

The truth is, while you may no longer love your wife, you do love the family you created together and it's for them that you need to be in your masculine now, while you find a vessel for your vulnerability.

This vulnerability is a human quality that we all have, but us men have been conditioned to maintain that stiff upper lip. To suppress our emotions and never cry, which is crazy because the weakness is in bottling it all up and not letting it out. That's the stuff that will make you ill. Crying can empty a space for us to eventually fill with happiness.

In the beginning of a divorce a man will normally slip into one of two states. Victim mentality or suppression, neither of which help him in any way. What's needed is something in the middle, where you can still have all the emotions, but learn how to express them better and the first step to that is by being vulnerable with yourself. If you feel sad, then cry. Why on earth would you not do it if your body is telling you to? Obviously, if you're on a train or in the middle of a supermarket then it's not ideal, but you get my point. One thing I can tell you, and it's as true for women as it is for men, a good place to start is in the shower. If you feel that tightening in the throat don't try to suppress it, it's there for a reason. When you lose your marriage, even if you were unhappy in it and you were the one who instigated the divorce, you still undergo a series of physical and emotional effects that are part of being human. It doesn't matter how long your marriage lasted, you were part of a couple and every single decision you made throughout it has involved the other person somehow. Now everything has changed and your neural pathways are confused – this is science not mumbo jumbo. Your neurons are firing on the couple relationship still and so they search for the normality of that. If they can't find it, they will keep searching and this is why a lot of men jump so quickly into new relationships after a divorce; it's a psychological response. Before you do that, just hit the pause button for a while and think things through. It will definitely be in your best interest to do so.

Divorce signals the death of your marriage and as with death in the traditional sense, you will go through the five stages of grief.

- DENIAL
- ANGER
- BARGAINING
- DEPRESSION
- ACCEPTANCE

During this period of time, no matter how long it lasts, you will need to find a way to deal with your vulnerability effectively and the best way to do that is to find a safe container for it. The key here is in finding a person or space where you can let go safely and openly. The best outlet for your grief is a space where it won't find its way back into the process, so you want someone who does not have a vested interest in what is happening. Your family and friends, the ones who love and care for you most, will all have a vested interest in you and your divorce and, to some extent, your work colleagues and boss too. On an unconscious level the advice they give you will be governed by the thoughts they have and if you have told them everything in your open and vulnerable stage, they will try to manipulate you on an unconscious level into making decisions and choices

that suit them, not you. There is no malice in them.
It's not intentional and they won't be conscious of
their manipulation, which is why I talk about finding a
safe container. These people really do want to help,
but they are not the people to share your vulnerability
with. Most of the time they want the best for you but
their best and yours will always be two different
things.

As I talked about in the previous chapter, you're
going to be a mass of emotions and it will be easy to
act on them. If you try to emotionally distance
yourself from your ex and shut down your feelings,
you can slide into focusing on any bad things she may
have done. This fits nicely into victim mentality and
becomes an easy choice to make as you can label her
the bad guy in all this. If you sit down and pick it all
apart, you'll find a lot of things to blame her for, then
before you know it, you're calling her a bitch. This is
really unhealthy and when you use your emotions
with words like that, you transfer your own shitty
feelings into blame and your ex becomes the target. It
may make you feel better for a brief moment but it's
not the long-term solution.

"When setting out on a journey, do not seek advice from those who have never left home."

Rumi

4 CHAPTER FOUR
SEEK ADVICE

Advice

noun

guidance or recommendations offered with regard to prudent future action.

"*my advice is to start with a free consultation*"

Ok so you're getting a divorce, but where the hell do you start? Let's talk about that ... it's likely you're feeling overwhelmed and definitely unprepared for what's to come. You might even be in a kind of shock; denial even, which can make you avoid doing anything practical at all. Burying your head in the sand at this time is the worst thing you can do because if you don't take the lead, your wife will.

Feeling a loss of identity can make you hesitate, not knowing what you should and shouldn't do, while at the same time you're trying to show the world that you're fine. You're coping. You're dealing with it like a man and you don't want to fall apart in a society that idealistically looks at men to be strong. Society expects the stereotypical strong and silent version of you, but you can't let that influence you because the way you deal with your divorce now will determine your future health and happiness. Don't buy into the version of you that society expects.

'Man up for God's sake'

If you hear that phrase from anyone, whoever it is, don't listen to them. They are not the person to be seeking advice from right now.

The decision to divorce has been made and so what's really important is to work out what comes next. As a man there's a lot to do but there's not a lot of advice out there for us men specifically, which makes the situation even more challenging. This is wrong and it's also one of the reasons why I'm writing this book. You're working toward the end of some thing not just one thing as divorce affects every aspect of what has made up life for you during your marriage.

Seeking advice is really important but I'll caveat that with this - not all advice is equal. If you asked the opinion of your divorced mate whose wife had been cheating on him for most of their marriage, the advice you'd get would be tainted by his experience. People, well-meaning or not, will have their own agenda and projections onto your situation. I see it in my

Facebook Group, The Modern Man Club all the time. The questions the guys ask are specific, but the answers have been dictated by individual perspective and there are always many opposing opinions because of that, like this one for instance:

"Don't do it like that mate, I did it that way and she took me to the cleaners."

The group is a great place for them to vent and share but the advice might often come from a skewed perspective. It's not solely about the advice though, it's more about having a place to hang out where you're understood. A place where there are common interests and you don't feel so alone. Men in general like to give advice. They like to fix stuff and come up with answers to help and this is essentially male bonding, so when you read or hear opposing answers, just be conscious that you don't let a personal perspective rub off on your actions. Individual opinions are always formed by individual circumstances.

Even though marriage vows are similar in most religions, no two marriages are the same. Each has its own set of circumstances that are unique to the couple in it, so when someone gives you advice based on their own experience, taking it would be like divorcing their wife, not yours.

When you start looking for help, start by looking to those who have no unconscious agenda for your divorce to serve. You might think a female friend is the ideal person to talk to as you've been friends for years and you have a great relationship where you can talk about anything, but we can never know anyone so intimately that we know what goes on in their head. What if that female friend always felt you'd be a great match for her single sister or her even? This is actually a really common scenario (for both sexes), so if that were the case here, the advice you'd get would be governed by her feelings, unconscious or otherwise.

If you have a sister yourself, you might consider pouring your heart out to her because she will have your best interest at heart. But she is genetically invested in your marriage and her advice will be governed by it too. Subconsciously, she may be swayed by her own relationship with your ex, especially if they are great friends, holiday companions or even work colleagues. Even your friends will have formed their own opinions about your marriage over the years and they will project their thoughts and feelings about your divorce into how they would do it themselves … but they are not you.

Honestly, the best advice I can give you at this stage, is to make use of the free consultations that most solicitors offer. I say this not to be cheap, but to help you get more than one professional angle on your situation. The law is the law, but each firm will have their own interpretation of how to use it when it comes to your situation. With this in mind, don't just book an appointment with one firm, visit a few to see who among them resonates with you most. These are free consultations, so you're under no obligation to make a commitment at the end of the session. Take a notebook or use your phone for notes to compare them all before you engage anyone and do take into consideration that a solicitor cannot advise on personality, so their advice will always be generic. This is about your marriage, your wife and your children and as you know them better than anyone, don't just take on board what a solicitor has said without thinking it through. Be in your masculine, trust yourself, don't be afraid to question the solicitor and do tell them if you've received conflicting or more favourable advice from another firm. Give everyone the opportunity to give you their best advice for you. Shop around. Listen to your gut. Trust your intuition and do apply logic, then remember to press the pause button before making a rash decision.

Always deal with the practical things first but also be mindful that none of it means shit if you're falling apart. If you feel like you are, do not ignore it and carry on because you think you have to. Seek help and look for a combination of advice, support and accountability to make sure you get the best kind of help for you.

Below are options that are available to you once you've made the decision to divorce and this list will help you get started.

SOLICITOR

Start by being practical and get a solicitor because then you will better understand the logistics and know where you are. A solicitor will help you understand both yours and your wife's rights. They can advise about property, money, family and changes you will need to make for any legal documents, such as a will, if you have one in place.

FINANCIAL ADVISER

A financial adviser will review your accounts and any assets and investments you have. There are many questions that need answers now and these are the most common:

- What am I going to do with my half of the money from the split?

- What will happen to my pension now?
- How am I going to make sure my children have a roof over their heads and I still have one myself?

If you're a businessman with your own business, at some point you may have given your wife shares or made her the Company Secretary. This has always been a popular way of doing things at company formation and if this is your circumstance, then get very clear advice about now.

COUNSELLOR

Want to get things off your chest? Booking a session with a counsellor is great way to do that. They will listen to you patiently as you tell them how you're feeling, and then help you understand where the feelings and problems come from. Counselling does not work on the root cause of it all though, so it is not a solution-based therapy.

CBT (COGNITIVE, BEHAVIOURAL THERAPIST)

CBT, as it is known, can help you with the way you think, and it can help you process your problems. It works on reframing your thoughts and it can be really effective, especially if you're feeling anxious, fearful or depressed.

HYPNOTHERAPIST

If you've only ever seen the TV hypnotherapists like the ones who get you to bark like a dog at the sound of a bell, I can understand why you'd feel apprehensive about this one. Hypnotherapy is used by many therapists, me included, as a way to connect with your subconscious mind and get to the root cause of whatever is troubling you. When they can get to the core of the problem, they use tools and techniques to help you overcome it. This helped me greatly when I was going through my divorce and I use my skills now to help other men going through the same difficulties. It's like taking your brain to the gym.

NLP PRACTITIONER (NEURO LINGUISTIC PROGRAMMING)

This is another practice I'm qualified in. NLP is a very effective way to help you connect your subconscious with your conscious. It focusses on the language of the mind and it can help you better understand your thinking, emotions and behaviour. This is extremely useful in helping you press the pause button too.

COACH

Coach is such a generic term and, if you look, you will find coaches for everything. This can make it difficult to find just one who will cover all that you need. For instance, a mindset coach can help you get focused on all you have to do, and an accountability coach can make sure you take action on it. Thinking about what you need the most help with will help you decide how to choose, but it's possible to book consultations with the ones you feel are able to help you best and then see who you resonate with. Coaches are usually multi-skilled but have trained for a specific purpose, like I did. A coach can be a great solution as they will choose a variety of methods to help you specifically, plus they are very forward focused which is perfect for when you need to set goals and plan for the future.

PERSONAL TRAINER

Many personal trainers are natural life coaches, being great listeners and really personable people. Getting in physical shape is proven to have a direct effect on your mental health which can only be a good thing right now and it will help you with your confidence when you are ready to get out there again.

The options above are not the only ones available to you, but they are the most commonly needed. They are taking care of the practicalities, but in addition to that, one of the best bits of advice I can give you now is around connection. When you start this whole divorce process you can lose your sense of belonging. Last week you were the man of the house and the husband but now you're in some limbo land and most likely feeling lost. If you can find a group where there are other men with a common interest, it will be a life saver. This is why I run The Modern Man Club. It's a safe space where men can come and hang out to discuss men's issues and there's absolutely no bongo banging involved.

"Put your children at the centre of your divorce, not in the middle of it."

Kate Anthony – The Divorce Survival Guide

5 CHAPTER FIVE
THINK ABOUT THE KIDS

End

noun

a final part of something, especially a period of time, an activity, or a story.

'the end of your marriage'

Endings are always going to be upsetting and a divorce is a big one. This is the end of your marriage but not the end of your family. Yes, you and your wife no longer love each other, but you still love your kids and they will play a big part in how you handle this divorce process. Their world is about to change and how they get through it is all down to what you and your wife do next.

In the worst-case scenario, when there's a limitation

placed on how often you can see your kids, don't let anger and bitterness seep into the relationship when you do see them. When you've gone from seeing them every single day to just at weekends or some other pre-arranged times, it can be heart-breaking for you all, but don't resort to blaming their mum for the lack of time you have with them or get into using them as pawns. Now, more than ever, they need security and stability. Focus on being a loving father and be the greatest example of a divorced parent you can be. The best way to teach anything is by example, so be respectful about their mum no matter what you're feeling yourself and give your kids your time, attention and the opportunity to talk about what's going on for them. Don't be tempted to overcompensate by spending too much money on them - what they need most is your time. Whatever you do or say now is likely to have an impact on their whole life, so show them what it means to be a good father and a good man in difficult circumstances.

When I was going through my divorce I listened to many podcasts in search of answers and one day I heard the best piece of advice that helped both myself, and my ex-wife think about how we handled the kids. I want to pass that on to you.

'Put your kids at the centre of your divorce, not in the middle of it'.

Kate Anthony – The Divorce Survival Guide

That hit home for me. It made perfect sense. I took it onboard, shared the concept with my ex-wife and this sentiment became our mantra. We both used it in every decision we made around the kids as the truth of it had totally resonated with us and if we found ourselves slipping, we reminded each other that the kids were our centre. On every decision we made around them we would ask ourselves: Is it in their best interest? This really worked for us.

We humans like to think we're good most of the time, but as humans we're all just trying to do our best. When the temptation is strong, it's easy to slip into using the kids as weapons but be mindful of the long-term effect this will have. Divorce can be a battleground and as men, we want to win the battle, but not at the expense of our kids. Sometimes it can happen accidentally, which is why it's important to try and pass on that concept and get some shared accountability around it.

The thing with kids is that they are very smart and will use your divorce for a little manipulation of their own. I don't know if you have any, or how old they are, but what I can tell you is they most likely knew you were getting a divorce before you did. My kids started asking if we were getting a divorce 3 years before we did. They'd picked up on the lack of connection between us long before we'd noticed.

As energetic creatures we can all sense these things, but over the years, as we grow into adults, we lose the ability to tune into them. As we get older, that sense is smothered by the busyness of life and we don't always notice things are really wrong until they are smacking us in the face. But our kids still have it and they pick up on energetic shifts as easily as they do hidden biscuits in the house.

It's a difficult time for everyone and your kids will not only be confused, but unaware of what should be shared and what shouldn't. When at your house or at home with their mum, they may see or hear things they don't have the maturity to know what to do about. Should they mention them or not? Are they secrets or not? They'll be afraid to share certain things from each household as they won't want to hurt either of you and they'll agree with whatever you say, even if they've already agreed the opposite with their mum. They might also be holding on to the hope that you'll get back together.

Whatever they do, they'll be doing it to protect you both. Just be aware that all of this is going on for them too and when it comes to getting something they want; they will use various tactics to get it -

"Mum is being horrible to me because."

When you hear something like that, your first response might be to get a little angry at your ex and often you'll compensate for it by letting your kids have what they're asking for. But your anger won't always end there and it can find a little trigger spot inside of you where it hides, just waiting for the right moment to react later. Kids don't mean to cause trouble, far from it, they just see an opportunity to get something they want, and they learn quickly how to play you off against each other.

The way to prevent this happening is by having a conversation with your ex in the very beginning; one where you agree to take a united front during this difficult time. It will be one of the best things you can do and it's also important to leave those lines of communication open with her. If you've not talked about it and a 'mum said' incident already happened, broaching the subject now needs a little tact and diplomacy. Keep your cool and be open to receiving information without feeling accused, even though it's going to be tough, it's for your benefit too.

If she sends you get a text message that pisses you off, don't reply by text, either press that pause button or try picking up the phone to hear her tone of voice as that text may have been misconstrued.

None of us are perfect and it's easy to slip into that kind of play. I catch myself even now … but the important thing is that I do catch myself and that's what matters.

Make a conscious decision not to do that and stick to it. Your kids will thank you for it one day.

"Values are like fingerprints. Nobody's are the same, but you leave them all over everything you do."

Elvis Presley

6 CHAPTER SIX
VALUES, VISION AND GOALS

Value

noun

principles or standards of behaviour; one's judgement of what is important in life.

"determining what has the most value to you to your life"

One of the positive outcomes of divorce is that it gives you an opportunity to re-evaluate your life and start to work out what truly matters to you. Instead of being caught up in the daily life you've known and continuing with those habits, you can think about making changes to better suit you now. Your health, your parenting and also what you want from a romantic relationship, can all be evaluated and improved upon now.

Once upon a time you bought into someone else's values and their vision, or you simply jumped on the bandwagon and started working toward the 4 bed semi, the 2 cars on the driveway, the big annual holiday, the weekend city breaks and providing everything the kids needed to grow into happy, employable human beings. Fulfilling society's dreams seemed almost expected of you, but did you get any satisfaction from it yourself? Think about it now - given the choice, is that what you would have done if you were thinking only about yourself and what you wanted out of this life?

This is such an important question to ask yourself now and the answers are so revealing. When I work with my coaching clients, I help them identify what is really important to them and while it's not surprising after all this time, it's sad to see just how many don't actually know what it is because they have been carried along for so long on someone else's dreams. If I asked you now to dig deep and think about your health, your career, the type of parent you want to be, how you want to be seen in the world and what you want to achieve before you leave it, what would you say?

You really need to take the time to think about these things. About you, your values and your vision because, if you don't, you will wake up in 10 years' time and think how the f*ck did I get here?

I remember in the early stages of my divorce I was sitting at my desk filling in some paperwork and I looked up at my vision board as if I were seeing it for the first time. I was looking at a big house in the country with horses on the land and I realised that none of it was for me. I had been visualising the future for my wife and children and I was working my arse off to achieve that life for them. There was not much of me up on that board at all and it was a revelation.

Who was I now? I'd come from a streetwise background and my future plans has all been pointing toward life in a country manor. Somewhere along the way I had lost a part of myself in the values and vision of my ex-wife, but she didn't force me to do that. It wasn't her fault it was my own doing.

Being a man involves owning who you are and it's important not to lose sight of that. I believe you can get to where you want in life if you work towards it, just don't forget where you come from and do make sure you're working towards your dreams - not just working to pay for someone else's. While I want good things in my life, I also don't want to forget my roots as they're an integral part of who I am and, if I'm honest, that can come in handy too.

It all comes down to being a man and what is expected of us. A man who is not achieving his goals will, at some point, feel like a failure. He will start to feel unworthy and can hit a downward spiral into victim mentality and appear needy. If you've had an acrimonious split, you have to turn this around otherwise your ex will continue to fire, she will be aiming at any past failures she can find, and this will push you deeper into a downward spiral. Take control of yourself now. Set goals that are solely for you, set your intention and then live by it. Let her see that you know who you are, that you have your balls back and that you will be conducting this process like a man.

During my divorce, I learned many things about myself and I learned some things from my ex-wife too…

A few months after we split, we met for lunch and as we were chatting amicably, she came out with:

"I'm proud of our marriage."

I thought about that. She was right and it was a really good lesson. Our marriage had been a success even though it was over now. For the majority of it, we did not struggle financially, and we'd raised our kids into great people. Yes, it ended, but doesn't everything? Sadly, we grew apart, but we also grew good humans and that is something we can congratulate ourselves for and be proud of.

After our conversation, I carried that philosophy into my dating life and because of it, I had some amazing encounters. All relationships have a beginning and an end but there are no rules as to how long they should last. Some of the dates I had after that were incredible. A short relationship that lasted 48 hours – the best 48 hours I'd ever spent with someone and yet never seen them again (by mutual agreement). Going into something like that requires honesty and you shouldn't be afraid of that because, believe me, not all women want to tie you down and have your babies. They have natural sexual urges too and they know what they want to satisfy them.

When you look up the word relationship it says:

The state of being connected

Nowhere does it say that connection should last forever.

'Successful people are simply those with successful habits.'

Brian Tracy

7 CHAPTER SEVEN
PICK A ROUTINE

Routine

noun

a sequence of actions regularly followed.

"I go to the gym every day instead of staying home alone and eating shit"

One of the biggest transitions you are going to make is living on your own again. That is going to be a big adjustment and it will most likely hit you on the first night, when you fall into a new bed and go to sleep alone … or try to.

Last week you woke up next to your wife, like you have done every day for the past 15 years. You got up, showered, dressed, headed into the kitchen and helped make the packed lunches as you grabbed coffee and a slice of toast. You left the house, spent the day at work, rushed home battling the traffic as it was your day to pick the kids up from school, then you made dinner while your wife helped them with homework. After that the evenings were normally spent watching a movie on Netflix. That was your routine.

This week you woke up to the sight of badly packed boxes at the end of a cheaply framed bed. You got up, showered and nipped into MacDonald's for a coffee before you went into work. At the end of the day you had several not so quick pints with the young lads from IT, got home, ordered pizza and, just because it was staring at you from the menu, some garlic bread too … and some chicken wings. You eat it while drinking beer from a foodless fridge and all the time you feel lonely. This is the stage of the process when it's easy to fall into unhealthy habits.

Now is the time to start as you mean to go on and you can use your masculine energy to do it. The primary driver for the feminine is security, but for the masculine it is challenge. Each morning when you wake up, you get to decide which energy to nurture. There is nothing wrong with nurturing your feminine but during this process you will need to be in your masculine energy and a great way to do that is to exercise first thing in the morning.

Make each morning purposeful and intentional and don't let your life become a reaction to how you feel.

You're are on an emotional roller coaster and it would be easy to slip into emotional eating, drinking or smoking. If you don't take control now, you could wake up in 10 years' time and wonder how you put on that 10 stone. How you became a 40-a-day smoker or how you ended up clubbing so much and are now suffering the bad health effects of the lifestyle choices you made.

But it doesn't matter how low you are feeling, you still have a choice and you can choose the good routines and habits that will help you get to where you want to be in the future. Think about it - what do you want now? Stop and consider your health, your wealth, your relationships and yourself, and create the habits that take you towards your goals.

If you don't belong to a gym, join one. Now that you're eating for one, you need to shop for one and trust me, that's not as simple as it sounds. A lot of what you buy will end up in the bin. Just think about lettuce; are you really going to eat a whole one? A lifesaver for me was finding Mindful Chef. Their one meal delivery boxes contained just the right amount of healthy food and I never had much waste. You don't find yourself overeating either, which is one of those bad habits you don't want to slip into. The meal boxes are an absolutely brilliant idea and should come with *suitable for newly divorced men* printed on the side!

Looking at the positive side of divorce, now is a great time for you to carve out the life you want. Make note of your existing habits and think about which ones no longer serve you. Had you got into the habit of going out a couple of times a week just to get away from the wife? Well you no longer have to do that, so think of a way to use that time for something else and make it something that will help you toward your goals. Make a long list of all the positive things you want to do; you want to be, and you want to have. Then create a routine that takes you closer to achieving them.

"Just because you desire something doesn't mean you value it."

Fidel Beauhill

8 CHAPTER EIGHT
RESIST THE REBOUND

Rebound

Verb

to spring back on or as if on collision or impact with another body

"to jump straight into a romantic relationship and collide with another body"

When you're hurting and feeling lonely the temptation to find comfort in sex can be very appealing. Most often it's not just sex, but feelings of romance and hope that you want, which, when translated, are simply feelings of not wanting to be alone, not having to feel rejected or not having to focus on the breakdown of your marriage. None of that is healthy. It's a way to heal your wounded ego and convince yourself that you are good enough and you are worthy of love.

If you've just left a long-term relationship, you won't have any idea of who the single you is, so what you need is time to rediscover him and find new independence. Otherwise, you might race straight into a new relationship carrying a lot of the past into it with you.

Summing it up poetically, I'd say, don't seek solace in the arms of another. Basically, the harsh truth is don't jump into a rebound relationship because it will be a mistake. If you've just left a long-term relationship, you have no idea who you are now and entering into a new relationship could be a disaster. It is finding out who you are that is important now and that is the key to how you best live the rest of your life from here on in.

Psychologically, when we come out of a relationship, our brain searches for a reference of who to be. We search for the last time we felt like ourselves; the last time we knew who we were. In most cases it takes us back to our youth - those carefree days when we felt invincible. When we were on the cusp of greatness and had the world at our feet. That is why a lot of men go back to partying and acting like they did in their youth.

In this situation you can be overwhelmed by different emotions and they can make you needy. It's then, when you're in your feminine energy and emitting look after me vibes, that this can be dangerous, especially if you come across a younger woman with a ticking womb. She will be drawn to that energy and she'll happily look after you and in doing so, fulfil her own need of becoming a mum. If becoming a dad again is not on your list, be really cautious and also consider the digital world we live in where everything is laid bare on for public consumption on social media. Think about how much harder all this will be when your ex sees these updates about you and another woman plastered about … and what about your kids seeing that too?

You may think you're looking for romance and romance will be everywhere because it's a billion-dollar business. The concept of romantic love is not even that old. Originally, marriage was a contract and the match was made by social standing, class or, at the very least, the hope that the man could provide an adequate life for the woman and the woman would provide heirs to carry on the family name. It was a trade and looks and chemistry didn't come into it. If they were there, it was considered a bonus.

Then in the 1930's a New York based Ad agency was hired by a diamond mine company, named De Beers and it was their job to come up with a way to sell the De Beers diamonds. The slogan they settled on was: A Diamond is Forever, which became their strapline and somehow the accepted ideal for the length of time a marriage should last.

The institution of marriage as we know it was the formal agreement to have sex and, in many countries, it still is. It's the western world that has capitalised on romance and used it as a tool. To get women to buy into the concept of one partner for life, romance was created ... and women bought it hook line and sinker.

So, what is romantic love? Well, if we look at it from that perspective, it's a multi-billion-dollar industry that has been 'Disneyfied'. But let's not be cynical and have divorce make us forget that it can also be the best feeling in the world. And let's also not confuse love with sex. Since the beginning of time there has been sexual attraction. It's a primal thing and if you're going to get real about who you are and what drives you, then you have to realise this.

Belgian therapist Ester Perel talks about us thinking that the quality of our marriage is dictated by the length of time we are in it. If you bought into the diamond is forever philosophy, then you'll understand Ester Perels' point. But if you look at the human race as a whole, primarily we are sexual creatures, not monogamous ones. The idea that marriage is for life is basically an advertising one

Getting back to who you are, at this stage of your divorce it's important you don't go back to the last reference point of view if that was in your youth.

Jumping into another relationship now won't help

you find out who you are and what you want out of life. Instead, you'll just repeat the same shit. Taking the time and doing the work on yourself will help you make your next relationship the right one for you. As a newly separated or divorced man, you won't be living to your values and making the right choices if you fall into a rebound relationship straight away. That doesn't mean you can't have sex – that is something completely different, but I'll get to that soon.

Let's talk about what's probably going on in your head. From a primal perspective our biggest fear is being shunned. Being outcast. This was a method of punishment for many years and it was seen as the ultimate punishment when you were banished from your community – expelled from the tribe as it were and sent away from everything and everyone you knew.

Now we see solitary confinement as the ultimate punishment for prisoners and this is deemed worse than hanging out with a bunch of rapists and murderers. This is because, as humans, we continually seek approval and validation. As a human race and at an energetic level we are all connected, so to be singled out and shunned would make anyone feel like there is something missing, which is why rebound relationships are common. When your marriage is over, you go looking for someone/something to fill the empty space.

Let me be blunt. I'm saying don't fall in love, don't move in with someone and don't get someone pregnant straight away. Sex is cool but be honest with yourself and the women you are interacting with because right now, you're at risk of confusing infatuation with feelings of love.

You may feel like it's the real deal, but you don't move out of a marriage and fall immediately in love with someone else. That is not love. It's a lot of other stuff going on there like ego and self-validation. Those gremlins in your head are telling you that this new person is going to give you all the stuff you're lacking because your ex is not around.

Ask yourself questions - Why the hell am I doing this? What am I getting out of it? Bring back that self-awareness and be honest. If you just want sex, then own that man. You've probably been in a sexless marriage for quite a while and you need to know that it's ok to go out and shag. Really it is. The whole women want to tie us down sentiment is bullshit but, to find that out, you have to step out of your people pleasing *Mr Nice Guy*. I'm not saying lie, definitely not. What I'm saying is be upfront and honest about what you want because you will find women who want the same.

If you go on dates as Mr Nice Guy, you may end up trying to mold yourself into what your date wants. You'll pretend to be whoever she is looking for and 6 months or a year down the line you'll be in another relationship that you didn't mean to get into because you were not honest, and you didn't want to break her heart. That would have been a mistake you could rectify easily enough, but not now she is pregnant and you're going to have another baby in your 40's, just when the youngest kid from your marriage is about to leave school. Is that really what you want?

Here's the thing … you don't have to do any of this if you just want sex. It's an assumption you're making. There are plenty of women out there who want what you want. They don't want to move in with you, they don't want to get married and they don't want you leaving your pants all over their floor.

If you're reading this and you've already met someone new, or you've met someone you have feelings for, just stop for a minute and drill deep into what you're really feeling. Don't just think you're falling in love. If you pursue it, you might wake up one day knowing you made a big mistake. Here's the thing; if it is love, then it will still be there when you've had the time to look at yourself and figure out what you really want. There is no rush. Press pause.

Before you jump into another relationship, figure out what it is that's making you feel like you want to be in one. Is it about external validation?

Are you worried about being alone and does that make you feel a lack of self-worth?

Do you think the world will think less of you as a single man?

Do you feel that being in a relationship is how you fit in with the rest of society?

Are you worried that you'll die alone sitting in an armchair with the dog at your feet?

If it's fear that's driving your need to be in a relationship, then that is total bullshit. For every elderly man at home with his dog is an elderly woman with her cats and, as a former will writer, I can tell you that there's plenty of sex going on between them, even in those situations.

The dying alone fear is a common one, but you can nip it in the bud because it really isn't true. There's a simple affirmation to help you overcome this one. Just wake up each morning, look in the mirror and say to yourself - *I AM NOT GOING TO DIE A LONELY OLD MAN.* You'll believe it, because it's true.

The best thing you can do at this stage is focus on

getting advice and doing the inner work on yourself, as this will help build the future you really want.

NB: While 'don't seek solace in the arms of another' is a term I use, I learned the concept from Dr Robert Glover, the author of 'No More Mister Nice Guy'. In his book he talks about building your cake, which is a powerful analogy and something I mention in this book.

I highly recommend you get a copy as I found it very helpful and I think you will too.

"The two most powerful
warriors are patience & time."

Leo Tolstoy (War & Peace)

9 CHAPTER NINE
TAKE TIME

Time

noun

the indefinite continued progress of existence and events in the past, present, and future regarded as a whole.

"if recovery takes time then so should you"

There's a psychological average to the amount of time you need to recover from a divorce, compared to the length of time you were married. It is 1 year to every 5, which means, if you're leaving a 15-year marriage then you give yourself 3 years to get over it.

Even if you've not been married that long, don't expect everything to be better in a few weeks. You've just undergone a major life change and, as with any change, it comes with a process that shouldn't be rushed. Think of it as an explosion that covered you in rubble and now, you're left trying to shake off all the dust.

You may think that if your divorce is amicable or if you know you no longer love your wife, you will be relieved when it's all over, but there are going to be unexpected feelings that crop up and catch you by surprise. It's going to take time to feel settled in yourself again because every decision you ever made in your married life has been thought through with other people in mind. Even the thoughts you took to be self-serving, like going on a golfing holiday with the boys. When you were making arrangements for that you would still have had to agree dates around birthdays, anniversaries, school holidays, childcare, appointments and exams, for instance.

I mentioned Dr Robert Glover in the previous chapter and I really got a lot of clarity from his 'cake concept'. This is his metaphor for life, and he talks about building yourself a beautiful cake and inviting the woman to become the cherry on top. When I first read his book it felt like a sucker punch and I remember thinking – do I really do that? The fact is, I had been doing just what he was talking about and it was quite a painful experience reading that and realising it was true. But the beauty of the book is in the simple concept. You, as a man, build the ideal life for you and you build it first before you even think

74

about getting deeply involved in a relationship with a woman. If that relationship doesn't work out and she leaves, you still have the amazing cake that you took the time to make. The ingredients of your cake are made up of what Dr Glover calls co-operative reciprocal relationships. This is your support network of professionals, family and friends who provide you with all the mental and emotional needs for you to live a beautiful and fulfilled life.

For me it's important to be independent and know how to fill my own bucket and, to do this, I need to be in my own power. This is something I have built and now I have a network of people who give me all the stuff I need, and who also support me as I support them. I say need because it is. I need these people around me, as do you.

When you first split with your ex you will have all this freedom to make decisions based purely on what you want. At first it might feel indulgent and exhilarating, which is when it's easy to spiral out of control. Best to assume nothing, take each day as it comes and don't forget those 5 stages of grief:

- Denial
- Anger
- Bargaining
- Depression
- Acceptance

These will affect every decision you make and every action you take. Life is going to change dramatically … be prepared for it.

There will be social events and gatherings that you would have been invited to as a couple, but you'll find all that has changed now. Say for example, your best couples' friends are having a birthday party for their 5-year-old daughter next week. They won't think twice about inviting your ex-wife because a single woman at a kid's party is totally natural. She can play with the kids without coming under any kind of scrutiny at all … you know where I'm going with this, don't you? Lightbulb moment here. A single man playing with a 5-year-old girl or even just being at her birthday party is simply not done and, as unfair as that is, it's how the world sees it and you are going to have to get used to things like that now.

The friendships you made with the other husbands are now shaky and it's most likely you will be the one to walk away. It's not all depressing though because on the positive side, you now have the time and opportunity to grow your own friendships with other men and that is a primal thing. It's something we were born to do. When we were little playground warriors, we wrestled and built camps in the woods. We used pocketknives to carve our names in the trees and we climbed, swam and ran like the wind together. Remember how good that felt?

Now as an adult you can't just go up to another bloke and wrestle him to the ground, but that energy is still there and you can use it in a different way, like organising a five-a-side football match or something like that. What's interesting to see is that contact sports are on the rise, particularly Brazilian Jujitsu which is very much like wrestling. Taking part in contact sport has given men the opportunity for non-sexual contact and it's definitely needed. This is tapping into a primal need that has been lost for too long.

The need for contact is where the danger lies in jumping into a new relationship. No matter what you think, or what you're thinking with when you first split with your wife, you really are not ready for a relationship. The time you have now would be better spent building up your support system.

You can feed yourself with female friends, family, professionals and most definitely boost your connection with male friends, so that you are not needy. This is a marathon, not a sprint and, that is why it's important to take your time and not shoot your bolt straight into the finish line. By doing that you carry your baggage in with you and in it are your greatest fears, which by the way are normally linked to our parents. We also bring our unique defence system against that fear - the Mr Nice Guy persona.

When I was younger, the fear I took into relationships was that I wouldn't be able to make her happy and she would leave. My defence against it was to do everything for her and buy her anything she wanted as I thought that would make her happy. It's a classic mistake which actually has the opposite effect and makes you repellent to the opposite sex. This results in her not wanting to shag you even though she doesn't know why.

If her greatest fear is being dominated or abused, then her defence mechanism will be to shut down, wrap into herself and push away. You can normally tell this by her body language. If this had happened in a relationship back then, I would find myself doing even more for her, becoming almost overpowering in my need to make it all alright. But as she wouldn't understand why I was doing that, it would feel like domination to her, which is exactly what she was afraid of. It had a different intention and a different energy, but the behaviour around it was similar. With an ingrained trait like that, my MO was always to find an emotionally distant woman, who I could use my relationship toolkit on to try and make her love me. Mostly women will find this repellent and, of course, the further away they moved, the harder I would try. It's both complicated and stupid and if you've not figured it out like I have, you'll just keep repeating the pattern. Even with all my knowledge and self-awareness, there was one relationship where we both slipped into old patterns. The woman was very self-aware like I was, but we still did it and our relationship ended very badly because of that. At the time it was like watching a car crash in slow motion; we could see what we were doing wrong, but we couldn't stop it.

These traits are deeply ingrained in all of us and they start with the relationship we have with our parents.

If you don't take the time to figure out who you are and what you want out of life, and if you jump straight into a relationship like that, then you'll repeat those patterns over and over again. That's why the time now is such a great opportunity for you to figure out your shit. Find out who the new you is then dig deep into your values, your vision and your goals as you create him and all that he wants for the future.

"The hardest part about being in a new relationship is learning to fart quietly again."

Anon

10 CHAPTER TEN
DATING AFTER DIVORCE

Date

noun

a social or romantic appointment or engagement.

"Repeat after me - I'll date only when I'm truly ready"

This is too big a subject for just one chapter and I have a whole book planned for it in the pipeline, but I wanted you to have something to get you started, so here is an introduction to dating after your divorce.

Basically, you are either going to feel like a kid in a sweet shop or like a non-swimmer who is scared of the water. Don't worry, there are do's and don'ts that can help you navigate these waters. Let's call them metaphorical armbands.

My first rule of dating is always, know the purpose of a first date.

You may think that it's for you to try and impress the woman and ensure a second date. No, that's not it. The purpose of a first date is to ask the right questions.

When you go on a date, always be yourself. If you are lucky and as well as being a nice person, your date is also an absolute stunner, but she slurps each time she takes a drink and it's making you cringe, don't think it's something little that you can get her to change. You can't and seriously, she is not for you.

Your first date is about you investing your time to see if she is compatible with you. That includes her wants and needs too, so ask the questions you need to ask. Think about it, even at this early stage, could she be your cherry on top? If her slurping is driving you mad, that answer is no.

The need to be liked is a human quality but it doesn't mean you tying yourself in knots to fit into someone else's box. If you fancy the pants off her, but she is talking about reggae music and saying she loves it so much that she plays it from morning to night; don't be drawn in by your urges here if you hate reggae music, because she is not going to change. Can you imagine a year down the line when you're eating your cornflakes to the sound of easy skanking … again? You will to want to pick up a hammer just to make the noise stop. That of course is an exaggerated example, but you get my point, don't you?

Be yourself – your whole self, and not some watered-down version of you that you bring out to impress, or even worse, not offend. Have the balls to be honest and truthful in your conversation and pay attention to the things you don't really like about her. Things you would want to change. These things will become the pebble in your shoe that grows bigger over time.

What you are looking for is the person you don't want to change at all. As Albert Einstein once said:

'Men marry women with the hope they will never change. Women marry men with the hope they will change. Invariably they are both disappointed.'

With that in mind, the best place to start is when you're sure you're ready. I said earlier that spending time with your male friends is one of the best things you can do when you're going through a divorce and it's vital, because you need to top up the masculine energy which has been depleted. As modern men, we've had our caveman beaten out of us and that's ironic when you think about it.

Taking it right back to basics, it was all about sex and there was an honesty to that. The strongest man got the girl – it was that simple. But it wasn't just because he was the strongest man and he could pick her up and carry her off, it was also because she saw him as more desirable because he could win the fight. It's why so many women are drawn to the bad boys.

Somewhere along the way, we men stopped the physical contact with each other, and our generation has missed out on it, unless you've been a rugby player. If you think back to the wrestling in the playground that I talked about earlier, it was non-sexual contact that was always part of the brotherhood and the camaraderie that came from friendship and trust in those you spent a lot of time with. This is crucial to a man's growth and it's a similar bond that you have with your family - knowing they are there no matter what gives you confidence and it's the same with your male circle of friends. Knowing they are there helps to keep your masculine energy strong.

To keep my own energy strong, I like to box. I get in the ring, get punched in the face by my opponent, maybe land a few punches myself and afterward we hug and congratulate each other on our skills. As men, our connections are strengthened by physical, non-sexual contact but when I'm done, I don't walk away filled with aggression, I walk away invigorated with a sense of achievement and pride in myself and at how my fitness and skills are improving. That is me in my masculine energy.

Now, when getting ready to date, knowing who you are, feeling strong and having had your masculine energy topped up, is how to get yourself ready and full of the confidence you need to just be yourself.

When you've meet someone and you know you want to date only her, ask the right questions as that will help you stay in your masculine in the future.

What don't you eat? Is a great one because if you know the answer you will know where not to take her. You know you want to see more of her, so it's safe to say you'll be booking restaurant tables at some point and knowing that she is a vegan will prevent you from taking her to the steakhouse and feeling awkward about it. If she is a vegan, then you'll be on safe ground practically anywhere as most restaurants have vegan options now. Being prepared means you can take charge and arrange the date, knowing you've got all angles covered.

Do be considerate of her, think about where she lives and choose a restaurant near that because if the date goes tit's up, she'll want to get home fairly quickly and if you've dragged her over to your side of town it will be an expensive taxi ride home. Worse still, you may be driving her as it doesn't matter if you've fallen out or not, you're a gentleman and you'll want to make sure she gets home safely.

Think about the time of year. Is it summer or winter?

Is it the rainy season? Do you offer to pick her up or order a taxi for her? These are things that you, as a man, think about but there's absolutely no need to discuss them with her as you are taking the lead and all she needs to know is that you've made the date as comfortable for her as you can. This you can do by taking into consideration all the aspects. It doesn't mean you don't make choices for yourself – you do. It's simply about being decisive and by considering her feelings without making them a priority.

This is consideration not empathy. Empathy is when you take on her emotions and they get mixed up with yours, which then affects the decisions you make. That will come across as flaky and wishy-washy and it makes you look like you're indecisive if her emotions don't fit with your core beliefs. To make this simpler - consideration is more cerebral and empathy is more emotional.

Like I said, this is a big subject, but these tips will help you get started. I had, and am still having, a lot of great dating adventures and I've got some of the best advice to share with you yet. But let's get the divorce done and get you living life as the man you want to become and next time, we'll go dating…

"No one can tell you what goes on in between the person you were and the person you become. No one can chart that blue and lonely section of hell.

There are no maps of the change, you just come out the other side ... or you don't"

Stephen King

10 CHAPTER ELEVEN
WHAT NO-ONE TELLS YOU

Tell

verb

communicate information in spoken or written words.

"*someone really should tell you these things*"

"*I throw some things into my holdall, not really thinking straight and I call my mum. She picks up after 3 rings … she knows.*

I walk into the lounge. Daughter number one is on her mobile. Daughter number two is doing her homework … I normally help her with that. They both look up and then at the bag in my hand. I feel tears coming.

My soon to be ex-wife is in the kitchen. I grab both daughters, hug them too tight, smell their hair and turn around to leave, but Revel our bulldog is at my heels. I keep going.

As I get in the car, I just sit there for a minute looking at the house that is no longer my home. What have I done? But I know it's the right thing to do and so I put the key in the ignition and drive…"

The purpose of this book is to help you remain strong throughout your divorce. To help you prepare for the road ahead and to successfully lead the way. But I want to be totally upfront and honest with you here as to what to expect … these are the things no one prepares you for.

Number 1 - Where do you stay?

Most of us end up at mum's house. If your parents still live in the house you grew up in, you'll be in your old single bed, although I'm sure the posters will have gone. This would be ok if it were just for a couple of nights, but it's not. You're likely to be there until the details of your divorce are sorted out into who gets what and that could take some time. So, what happens when you start dating? If you get to the stage where you'll be having sex, imagine how you will feel bringing her home to your mum's house.

You may feel ashamed that you're a mature man living with your parents, but it's a really common situation and an understandable circumstance, so don't let it bother you. Just own it because there is nothing embarrassing about it. It's a temporary situation. There are plus points too in that your kids will love to visit as they have you and their grandparents under one roof.

Number 2 – How do you go about dating?

If you do start dating and you use a dating app, what do you do when you see your ex-wife's friends online? If you are seeing them, then they are seeing you and that could get difficult. If it's just about sex, you'll be able to find sites that are specifically for that purpose and it's unlikely the friends of your ex will be on it. This is something to think carefully about and plan for when the time comes.

Number 3 – Where do you put all your stuff?

When you get a place of your own, the chances of it being a family sized home are slim. Most often you will end up in a flat and, while size won't enter your head in the beginning, you'll soon realise it when you're trying to squeeze your golf clubs into the one cupboard that is already acting as a coat rack. Think about options – is there an attic at your mum's? Are there things you can sell or donate to charity? This can be tough if you dwell on it and start think about all that you used to have, so knowing this in advance will help you prepare and plan for it.

Number 4 - Soft furnishings.

I had to include this because how the hell would we know anything about curtains? And what about that box thing that holds cutlery in the kitchen draw. And lampshades? For most men this is alien stuff, so if you do have a sister or a female friend, ask them to help you with these things. It's just easier and I can pretty much guarantee they will love helping you.

When I moved into my flat it took a lot of getting used to. I was low in energy and mindset and when I looked around me, I just didn't love anything about it. It was a friend who told me about some process, and for the life of me I can't remember the name now, but it was all about changing how you feel about your possessions and your surroundings. Here's what I did to change those feelings.

Each morning when I got up, I went around the house and stroked the walls (yes seriously). I said good morning to the flat, picked things up and let them bring me some kind of joy at the sight or feel of them. I also decided to add to the idea and charmed my flat as if she were a woman. As crazy as all this sounds, after a few weeks, it started working. There is a science behind it, in that everything is made up of energy, including us. Energy can be light or heavy and the last thing you need at this time is a heavy energy around you as it will wrap you up in a cocoon of depression. If you're in this situation, give it a try – no one will see you and what's the worst that can happen?

Number 5 – What if your ex starts dating?

Everyone's circumstances are different, but there may be times when you have to visit the family home. But what if your ex has moved on and started dating? Whatever your reason for being at the family home, you are going to notice little changes. Maybe an overnight toiletry bag in the bathroom or a pair of slippers next to your ex-wife's in the hallway. These little signs can trigger big emotions and you might start to think about your replacement parking his car in your spot or sleeping in the four poster you had bought with your bonus money one year. It's easy to become consumed by these thoughts and it's got nothing to do with the parking space or the bed at all but more to do with him taking advantage of your hard work. Listening to your self-talk and dwelling on things like this is the absolute worst thing you can do. By being aware of why you are feeling what you are feeling, you can rationalise these thoughts and prevent them from driving you crazy.

Number 6 – What about your pet?

The family pet was your dog before the kids came along. You've been his master for the whole 9 years and you've had him from a puppy. The girls are not walking him, your ex-wife says she is too busy, and it's not been great for you going there just to walk him every day, so now he lives with you in a flat with no garden. This happened to me and Jackson. I loved that dog. He really got me through it when I was spiralling down and it took around a year before I got my energy back. In that year I kept a journal every day and I'd grade myself by energy and what percentage I was feeling – it was eye opening to see the draining effect divorce had on me. One morning I woke up and felt like I was through the other side and I graded myself 100%. When I looked at Jackson that morning it was like he knew. It was like he'd seen me through the whole thing and now his job was done. That's when he left us and that hurt a lot. A pet is just like a member of the family and they too are affected by your divorce.

There are so many things to think about, but you can't take them all in at once. What you can do at this stage is work through the chapters in this book. I've made it small so it's easy to carry around with you and when you need some non-judgmental support, open the pages or come and join The Modern Mans Club … I'll be there with a virtual bear hug for you.

EPILOGUE

We are modern men – a breed that has never been before, which is why the same old stale advice out there is not for us. It's time to write some new rules because the old ones are no longer working.

Doing the work that I do opens my eyes to the seriousness of the situation we find ourselves in. The men only spaces that previously existed have gone and I understand why, because they were built on outdated rules – The No Women Allowed was signage all about male dominance back then.

The golf course and the boxing ring were places men could compete and celebrate together afterwards and the football ground was where they could be part of a gang in support of a united cause. If you've ever sat in the stands you will know the absolute joy and exhilaration of cheering in unison with 40,000 other supporters as your team score a goal. It's as close to heaven as you'll get … without a woman.

These traditions create bonds and these bonds create a brotherhood, yet while these places should not exist to promote exclusion or dominance, they should still exist. The antiquated male only space has gone, and rightly so, but there has been nothing since to fill the void and that is one of the biggest problems, we, as men, face today.

The gap that remains has been filled with loneliness, self-esteem issues, unhappiness and deteriorating health. In it, there are men who have given up on their hopes, wants and dreams and they are wandering around lost in an identity crisis.

At a primal level, losing touch with each other makes us forget what we really are and when we do that, we're no longer sure of our place in the world.

We live in a world where loneliness is the number one problem for men of our generation and that frightens me. I had zero idea of just how many men feel alone - especially when they go through that divorce and come out the other end with no close mates to hold space for them. Yes, that's a very female term, but what it means is a non-judgmental friendship and a place to go in times of trouble – in other words, your safe container. This is what women do so well for each other and that is why there is so much out there in support of women now.

These sisters … or queens as they call themselves now, have stood up and put their arms around each other and it's been a wonderful thing to see. But what about us?

I think it's time we dusted off our own crowns…

ABOUT THE AUTHOR

Fidel Beauhill is a divorced father of 3 who grew up in seventies Britain with a Jamaican father and a British-Brazilian mother. He is a Coach and the founder of The Modern Man Club, a safe space where men can hang out and remember who they are.

As a former importer living in Spain, he and his family were living the life when the recession hit, and they lost everything. Moving back to the UK, Fidel grew a successful will writing business, working long hours to fund the dream, but on the cusp of divorce, overweight and in financial trouble, he found himself lying outside his front door having had a suspected heart attack. It was then he decided that his life had to change and so he got more serious about his boxing and started on a journey of self-development that led him to his purpose in life.

A child of divorce himself, Fidel's parents split when he was 7 and he remembers his father as being a dignified and consistent presence in his life. He also credits him with being the original Modern Man … the spark that ignited Fidel's purpose.

He now uses all that he learned throughout his own divorce, training and the lessons from his father to inspire positive masculinity in men and rebalance the status quo.

Printed in Great Britain
by Amazon